The Colors of a Life

Rachel Toalson

Other Books by Rachel

Poetry
this is how you know
Life: a definition of terms
The Book of Uncommon Hours: haiku poetry
Textbook of an Ordinary Life
this is how you live
Sincerely Yours
Textbook of a Parenthetical Life
Textbook of an Extraordinary Life
this is how you fly

Essay
Parenthood: Has Anyone Seen My Sanity?
The Life-Changing Madness of Tidying Up After Children
This Life With Boys
We Count it All Joy: Essays
Hills I'll Probably Lie Down On
If These Walls Could Talk
The Days are Long, But the Years Are Short
Life's Little Lessons: 100 Micro Essays

To see all the books Rachel has written, please click or visit the link below:

www.racheltoalson.com/writing

The Colors of a Life

BATLEE
PRESS

Published by
Batlee Press
Post Office Box 591484
San Antonio, TX 78259

Copyright ©2025 by Rachel Toalson
All rights reserved.
Printed in the United States of America.
Interior design by Toalson Media.
Cover design by Ben Toalson. www.toalsonmarketing.com

No part of this book may be reproduced or transmitted in any form or by any means, electronic or mechanical, including photocopying and recording, or by any information storage and retrieval system, without permission in writing from the publisher. For information regarding permission, write to Batlee Press, PO Box 591484, San Antonio, TX 78259.

The author appreciates your taking the time to read her work. Please consider leaving a review wherever you bought it and telling your friends how much you enjoyed it. Both of those help get the book into the hands of new readers, which is incredibly important for authors. Thank you for your support.
www.racheltoalson.com

Names: Toalson, Rachel, author.
Title: The colors of my life / Rachel Toalson
Description: First edition. | Batlee Press, Texas:
Batlee Press Books, 2025

10 9 8 7 6 5 4 3 2 1

First Edition—2025

*For Ben and J, A, H, B, Z, Ash
who bring infinite color
to my life*

Introduction

I've spent years thinking about my history—the people and places I come from, the experiences that shaped me. The full-color memories that made me who I am.

As I thought about this history, of course, I felt compelled to write about it.

Not every poem in this book is a memory of the distant past; some of them are memories of a more recent past. What they all have in common is that they are memories that have infused my life with brilliant color. The people in them, the places that made their mark, the lessons I carried away from those rich and colorful experiences—I remember them for a reason.

As I thought of the particular colors saturating my memories, I found myself paying more attention to my present life and the kaleidoscope of colors that exist in every moment. So often we let life slip us by, caught in our varying shades of distraction. But noticing something as simple as color—that made all the difference.

What is color? Light. What is life without color? I don't think I want to know.

Color might have shown me how to live.

The past, braided into the present, braided into the future.

Life is a vibrant rainbow, isn't it?

Not all these colorful memories are happy and sweet. Some of them are somber and somewhat melancholy. But life needs every color to shine and sparkle. So I—we—embrace them all.

In these pages you'll find humor, introspection, love, hope, and so much more. You'll find past braided with present and future.

You'll find the color of my life. And, I hope, some colors of your own. A world of brilliance, wonder, and beauty.

Thank you for reading.

Green

Searching for Four Leaf Clovers

We looked for them
thinking we could change our luck

every dark patch of grass
a possibility for treasure

I'd sit there for hours
combing through the tangled stems

sifting through three-petaled clovers
begging the universe to send the magical one

what would I have done with it
if I'd found it

probably I would have asked luck or
fortune or the magical four-leaf clover

to bring my dad back home
where he belonged

I spent hours running my hands
through unlucky specimens

but I never found

what I was looking for

Neither did
my dad

Fashionable Statements

The shirt wasn't all that flattering, even
but that wasn't the part
that really mattered
What mattered was
the Tommy Hilfiger logo
What mattered was what it said:
I was not a charity case
I was someone who had money
to splurge on a Tommy Hilfiger shirt—
two of them, actually,
same style polo in
burgundy and green

>   (They didn't have to know
>   I'd worked two whole 4 a.m.-to-close shifts
>   to buy them)

I spent years trying to prove
I was someone other than
myself

What I Didn't Have Warped My Vision

I wasn't jealous of who they were

for the most part
I liked who I was

I was jealous of what they had

it's not that they were well off
or had nicer things than I did

I didn't even know details like that
about their lives

but I did know one thing they had
that I didn't

and it meant the divide between us
reached the depth of jealousy

because maybe I would have
given up who I was for what they had

or maybe not

who's to say what a girl would trade

for her dad

The Interior Decorating Mystery

What was the point of that green carpet
stretched across the floor of a
screened-in porch
looking and feeling
just like astroturf?

It was a place she sat
smoked
watched the neighborhood goings-on

but concrete or carpet-green Astroturf
it wouldn't have mattered

Maybe it was another mystery
hidden behind the
shiny fake facade of family

How many secrets had she buried under that green?
How many more lived in her basement?

How many would it take to explode the world?

How to (Accidentally) Kill a Plant

It's not purposeful
or personal

They start out well,
green leaves open and healthy

The first week we forget to water them
they hold on, still green,
still standing tall

The second week we forget to water them
they bend a little, ends turning yellow,
some of the leaves curling in on themselves,
probably for self-protection, poor things

The third week we forget to water them
their edges shrivel up into brown crusts,
leaves droop like hanging heads,
green turns to a sickly yellow

And by the time someone realizes
they should water the plants,
there's no telling whether brown
will turn back to green or
leaves will lift or we'll ever see

one of those white flowers again

I Found My Power in Marching Band

I didn't care
what happened out there
on the field,
I just wanted to
make it to half-time,

when Mr. Dubose would
wave us down to the track,
we'd line up in our places,
and I got to lead
the marching band,

on top of the world
for seven minutes
every Friday night,
from September to
November.

We Called it The Boat

it was big, square,
commanding our
entire driveway

we never fought about
who sat where
the backseat rose taller
than the front
passengers given a
perfect view of the world
outside the windshield

we never wore seatbelts
slid across the backseat
into each other on every turn
some days giggling about
the invasion of space
most days shoving
each other away

it was always an adventure
riding in that giant car

we were almost as sad
to see it go

as we were
to see him go

The Eyes Don't Always Tell the Right Story

What did it mean,
        the crinkling?

They'd crinkle
when he was amused,
tiny wrinkles folding in the corners,
sometimes accompanied by a laugh,
though I can't remember
what it sounded like.

They'd crinkle
when he was furious,
squinting down his nose,
examining the specimen before him
as though it weren't
his daughter.

They'd crinkle
when the judgement came down—
    in your room
    wait for me
and when he came in
    snapping that belt
and when he said those words
that always preceded the punishment—

*this will hurt me
more than it hurts you.*

They'd crinkle
when he lied.

They say
if you want to know
what someone's thinking or feeling,
just watch the eyes,
but I never learned a thing
from my father's.

The Great Escape

We used to run those fields
like they belonged to us

bare feet pounding prickly grass
trampling stone-like holes of giant ants

dodging cows that eyed us warily
only stopping to examine

a knobby backbone or a skull
sometimes picking them up

carrying them all the way to
the tree at the end of our world

where we'd stop, climb, rest our heads in crevices
that belonged most of the time to birds

who never paid any attention
to those chalky white animal remains

we propped on branches
to say, *This is mine*

to say, *I was here*

to say, *Just don't forget me*

We ran to get away
We ran to be free

We ran to find peace from yelling,
slamming doors, sour-scented words

We ran to believe
we could run

Who Do You Think I Am?

say you grew up in
a house surrounded by cornfields
and people have an idea
a preconceived notion of
who you are—

small-town girl
conservative values
probably a bit empty-headed
or maybe just convinced
of ludicrous things
she probably doesn't
even think for herself

but the truth is
I stared long and hard
into those cornfields
I took note of their ears
and I learned to listen
but probably the most
important thing is
        I learned
and so I came to
think for myself

and though I hid
from those cornfields
for longer than I can remember
I also came to realize
that they never lost me
as I supposed

they found me

Pink

Proof

Every spring
the fields filled with buttercups,
pale pink petals cupped around
a powdery yellow middle.
I'd pick one,
tuck it behind my ear,
pick another for my mother,
and pick a third to rub on my forearm,
all the way across,
a fine streak of yellow.
I did it for no other reason
than to prove I had not,
as life had begun to whisper,
faded into
invisibility.

Red Vs. Pink

Some use a red pen,
but red pens shout
    Fix this!
    Mistake!
    Imperfection!

I edit with a pink pen;
a pink pen says
    Here's an improvement
    to your piece, which is
    already lovely but which
    needs a slight adjustment
    here and here and
    here here here here here here here

Pink is Freedom

Did I miss out
on not having
a daughter?

Probably,
but I try not to
dwell on that

I have sons
and not one of them
is afraid to wear pink

it's ridiculous to
put genders into
colors

outrageous to set up
those boxes
that say

sons will leave you
but daughters will
become your friend

who's to say one of my sons

won't become a friend
later in life

who's to say
they won't stay right
here

who has the right to say
only girls wear
pink

my sons wear
all the colors of
the rainbow

maybe the world
will try to tape them up
in their boxes

but I hope they break free
I hope they keep embracing
the rainbow of possibility

I hope they wear their pink
shirts shorts pants socks glasses shoes
and they don't even notice

the people
who might look
twice

Not All Questions Are Created Equal

It's funny to think
that once upon a time
we used to wear
matching pink dresses
     white hats
          shiny white shoes
and hold the same little baskets
tied with pink ribbon,
picture perfect girls for the
obligatory Easter photo
followed by the
obligatory Easter service
at the church down the way
followed by the
obligatory Easter lunch
with family.

We got all the candy
we could eat
for our troubles.

Thirty-some years later
we hardly talk,
and all we get for our troubles
is a little question that

sneaks in when you
least expect it:

> Why don't you ever call
> your sister anymore?

Corrections

pink bleeds everywhere

you've been over this
so many times

you didn't think the pages
would have so many cuts
but that's the way it goes

every time you read a manuscript
you're in a different place
a different mindset
it stands to reason
you'd change things

that's why there's pink everywhere
you tell yourself
but you see the typos too—
just a few, but enough

how do you catch them all?
you might read it forever
and never find every one

nothing's perfect

somewhere in the finished
black and white of
a published book
you leave a little pink mark
Granddad should be Grandad
and you hope no one else
will ever notice

I Never Could Get Rid of Her

I had friends

I was the kind of kid
who made them easily

but my best friend
wasn't a person
she was a doll

I'd had her for as long
as I could remember
a gift when I was a baby

her hair testified to my love
no longer smooth and silky
but gray and knotted up
into short balls

the eyelashes of one eye
fell off in my brother's hand
(or so he claimed)
so she always had a
sleepy-eyed look
when lying flat
peering at me from one eye

her head separated from her body
on more than one occasion
so my great-grandmother
sewed a new body
fluffy and shaped like
a gingerbread man
attached it to her head with
giant Frankenstein stitches

the pink of her lips had scratched
almost completely away

I didn't care how ugly she was
she was my Sally doll
her plastic face helped me fall asleep
the back of one hand pressed
to her cool cheek
I'd sink into dreamland
before her cheek turned warm
even on the nights I could hear
my mother and father arguing
through the walls

She's still in a box somewhere
in one of my mother's closets
a reminder that childhood

never really leaves us

Compositions

They stopped selling
my composition books at Target

I write everything in these books,
fly through ten or more a year,
and now they're obsolete

I can't believe
I'll have to change
what I've been doing for so long

I have one book left
in my supply stash and then…?
I try to avoid the question

I'd like to believe
this isn't the end of
my writing career,
but careers have been lost
over less

No, I'll figure something out,
I always do, but I'll sure miss
the perfect brilliance of
that pink cover

Multiplicity

Do you think you can fix it?
he says one more time.
I haven't answered him
the last two, because I don't like
making promises I can't keep,
and he hates the word maybe.

He has another stuffed animal
that needs stitching, this one
a tiny keychain leopard that
wouldn't need more than
a stitch or two.

There's a collection
of stuffed animals
in need of fixing
piled on the floor of my closet,
stacked up beneath my sewing table.
I don't have time to sew anymore.

Be careful, his older brother warns.
*I gave her some stuffed animals
to sew up years ago, and
I never got them back.
They disappeared.*

He takes back the pink leopard,
clips it on its ring.
He'll take his chances
with a rip.

Sometimes I wish
there were
three of me.

The Power of One-Sided Conversations

He talks and he
talks and he talks
I stare and try to follow
The conversation takes me
back to when he was a boy
prattling on about Minecraft
and Basher books and
Bok Choy Boys

I want to listen
He rarely talks to me anymore
Mostly it's yelling
He thinks I'm an enemy
Nostalgia steals my attention
I see the tiny pink-faced newborn
the dark penetrating eyes
we called intelligent even then
the little nose I used to kiss
when he took naps in
the crook of my arm
He used to smile all the time
He rarely smiles now
Where did my little child go?

He finishes up

We go our separate ways
Maybe we'll meet again
sometime in the future

These Shoes Were Made for Running

they say you're supposed to ditch
them every four hundred miles or so

I'm not sure why
I kept these so long

they're not even
particularly comfortable

don't feel like running on clouds
like my more expensive pair

they're all worn down
in the familiar places

I guess the simplest
explanation is their color

they remind me of my
favorite part of the sunset—

that moment where the sky
turns blindingly pink

and you think

it's almost time to rest

Reminiscing

Back when life was simple
we wore pink hair bows
at the crowns of our heads,
loops flopping when we ran

Back when life was simple
we pushed the merry-go-round,
leaped on, watched the world spin
and held on for dear life

Back when life was simple
we walked all the way
across a highway to get to
the only convenience store in town
We stared at the candy for hours,
trying to decide which we wanted most,
the quarter in our hands
burning our palms
with excitement

Back when life was simple
we climbed the trains that stopped
across the street from our house,
explored every inch of them we could,
made sure to hop off before

they barreled to the next destination

Back when life was simple
we had a white dog who chased chickens
and dug holes and sometimes set off
the electric fence around the garden,
pursuing a rabbit
She disappeared one day,
but no one told us she'd
gone into the fields to die

Back when life was simple
we watched *The Goonies* and
dreamed about the kinds of treasure
we might find at the bottom
of the dirty lake down the road—
all we needed was a map
and a way in

Back when life was simple
we fixed those pink hair bows for each other
like we all deserved a crown

Sometimes I ache to live
back when life was simple

Gray

Gray Skies

I like them every now and then
those gray-skied days

but too many in a row
leave me feeling out of sorts

        overly tired
        a little down for no apparent reason

but I can't wish them away
forever

does anyone truly appreciate the sun
without the gloom?

Don't Let it Die

We still subscribe
to the newspaper.

It's not exactly
a millennial thing to do,

but maybe I'm a little
old-fashioned.

I like holding the tissue-thin
paper in my hands,

the black smudges of newsprint
staining my fingers,

watching my kids
huddle over the comics.

Even if I don't read it
start to finish,

if I only have enough time
to consume an article or two,

I faithfully pay my bill to have

The San Antonio Express-News

delivered to my
driveway.

Sons

it doesn't matter
how many pairs of skinny jeans
I put in their closet

how many nice shirts
I add to round out
the look

they will reach for
their comfy pants
every chance they get

until the knees are blown out
and they're two sizes
too small

not even school pictures
can change
their minds

if they had to write an ode
to the thing they love most in the world
it would be their gray sweatpants

The Cost of Living with Children

they're arguing again

I can hear them
through the closed door

I closed the door
because they weren't
getting along and
I wanted to mute
the discontent

my goodness they're loud

this time they're fighting
over a gray Lego piece
how many gray Lego pieces
do they have in their collection
        probably millions
but they only have one of
this particular gray piece
that looks like every other
gray piece

what's the difference

that's a loaded question
no sense asking
just shut the door
and turn on some music
and pretend you can't hear
raised voices bickering
about nothing

Tell Me What's In Your Purse

it was more a bag
than a purse
she stuffed it like her house
full of inexplicable things

maybe she wanted
to be prepared
maybe she forgot
what she'd put inside

she won every
baby shower game
that examined the
contents of a purse

she never went anywhere
without it
her security looked like
gray leather

it was as much a presence
as she was
tucked in a corner
watching

Imagination Will Take You Anywhere

we used to ride it like a horse
        that propane tank
it took some doing to
ready it for the rodeo

spiders liked to make
homes at its base
some days there were
hundreds of them
who knew where they relocated
when we brushed them aside
with a broom so we could
mount our bronco and
pretend we could
somehow escape the world of
        divorce
    a missing dad
and growing up

Questions I Think When Walking Around My House

It's funny, the things you miss—
he used to leave drawing pens
all over the place, their gray bodies
cast in varying positions,
wherever he'd last
stretched out to draw.
The pens have disappeared,
because he doesn't draw anymore.

Why doesn't he draw anymore?

Say Goodbye to a Piece of Me Too Small to Find in Sparkling Grass

You couldn't see the
clouds this morning
it was too early for the sun
to wake behind their curtain

but you could feel them
a certain heaviness in the air
my headlamp cut through mist
and I probably should have known
that didn't bode well

I didn't sleep much last night—
that's one excuse
Another: I was looking
for other things—
uneven places in the sidewalk
that might trip me up
I was thinking, *Pick up your feet*
I wasn't considering how best
to wipe away the moisture
collecting on my face

I suppose I should have been
paying better attention

you always see these
things in retrospect

I swiped at the side of my nose
my nail caught the diamond ring there
and out it popped onto the sidewalk
or into the sparkling grass

I tried to find it
but it was impossible
in the darkness

I left it behind and wished
I'd taken those looming clouds
as a premonition

The World Isn't Fair, But it Should Be

Dress codes are unfair, you know
Yesterday my son put on shorts
his grandparents gave him
they were way too short
they were the kind of shorts
that would have landed me
in those ugly community sweatpants
the office reserved for girls
who broke dress code
they were unisex sweatpants
but it was only girls who wore them
because only girls got
their shorts measured
he wore those shorts all day
no one said a word

This morning my son came to
the table with a shirt
his grandparents gave him
any time he lifted his arms
the skin of his belly showed
I said, *a girl would get in
trouble for that shirt*
why? he said
it shows skin when you

lift your arms
he shrugged and
wore it anyway
no one said a word

Those gray sweatpants
and sweatshirts handed to the girls
with skin-revealing shirts
and too-short shorts
were intended to limit distractions
and someone somewhere decided
only the female body is distracting

I bet we can all give
a good guess who

The Power of News

I still remember
the first day
I picked up the newspaper
and my byline was in it

the day I had my first
full-page spread

the day I landed
a slot on 1A,
the coveted position
of any important story.

It was all a thrill that
added up to
something significant.
It said, *You are a writer.*

•

When I hear people
talk about fake news,
I flinch.
When I hear them
bemoan the terrible,

dishonest journalists of today,
I bristle.
When I see them share
an inaccurate story,
supposedly informative,
from a web site that's hardly
more than a blog,
a collection of thoughts
from people who have
no training or knowledge
in the art and science
of reporting news,
I shake my head.

I remember it's not me
they're talking about.
I mean, it is,
but have you seen
what they think is news?

•

Some people think
the newspaper is on its way out.
Maybe it is.
But we still wait for ours,
especially every Sunday morning,

when we'll turn the pages
over tea and coffee,
when our children
peer over our shoulders,
when someone quietly steals
the comics and they crowd
in a corner to laugh and wonder
and touch the grainy pages
of newsprint.

They Call This High Intensity Interval Training

Do you imagine things
in the shadows?
I do. I see eyes of animals,
forms that turn out to be trees,
monsters that, on second glance,
are only my headlamp sweeping signs
or car lights illuminating the brush
on the side of the street.
My brain alerts me, my heart
pumps more blood to my legs,
and I speed past every
imaginary danger.

It's an interesting way to run
in the early, pre-dawn hours,
when most of the world's asleep,
except for an overactive imagination
and a hundred beastly shadows.

We Go Round and Round in Circles

Last night we had nine people
to take home in an
eight-passenger van.
We were only driving seven miles,
down back road stretches
with speed limits of
thirty-five miles an hour.
Our twins climbed in
the back hatch and tucked
themselves around boxes.

Do you remember? my mother said.
When your sister rode in
the back hatch that time?
We had a gray Ford Escort
that seated five, and we had
six people to take home
from a band concert.
My sister, the smallest,
climbed in the back hatch
and laid down flat.
We drove highways home,
listened to her roll,
laughed at what we might do
if we got stopped by a

well meaning police officer.
Keep your head down,
my grandmother told her,
*and hope he doesn't shine
a flashlight in the hatch.*

It was safer, certainly,
than the open bed of a truck,
and my mother had ridden in
plenty of those when she was a girl,
cruising down highways full speed.

My twins climbed out of the hatch
as soon as we got home.
Did you survive? my mother said.
We almost didn't, one of them said.
The fart smell's really bad back here.

They wished for the
open-air bed of a truck.

It's ironic how
the years turn
full circle.

Orange

Sweetness Only Lasts 'Til...

It was the one food
I would allow myself for breakfast—

the small orb of perfection,
tiny strings in the rind I would pull away.

I meticulously removed all the
white strings left on the fruit,

then divided it up,
slice by slice,

the cool sweetness of it
scrambling my senses,

as close to ecstasy as
an eleven-year-old could get

after a night
of fasting.

Twenty-five years later
they would tell me

my brother's brain tumor

was as large as a small orange

and I would remember
those breakfasts of long ago.

No longer sweet but
sour   bitter   unthinkable.

Ode to the Skinny Jeans

For Ben

There you are, looking so fine,
climbing all in and out of my mind,
pants so loud they steal my eyes
and arms so strong they agonize.

Won't you join me for a dance—
bust a move in tight orange pants?

Finding Nana

She never went anywhere without her orange lipstick.

I used to watch her put it on
in her big vanity mirror,
framed with chipped dark wood

She'd press her lips together,
then smile at the reflection.
I wondered even then why she chose orange.

Maybe she liked how bright it was,
the way it made her green eyes pop,
how it spoke a story of boldness with gentleness.

She thought red belonged
to a harlot,
orange was safer;

she would reapply it in the car before church,
and after eating at home,
and in front of the store.

She kept a tube in her purse
and would phone my mother
when she ran out.

I tried on her lipstick once,
and it made me look like a clown,
which only goes to show

there was never another woman like her.

Dodgeball

When the days turn warmer
and the heat inside our house intensifies

because of short tempers
and family togetherness

we take our
grievances outside:

In a wide blue bin is
an assortment of orange balls:

We line up on opposite sides—
kids on one, parents on the other:

The shout erupts us:
we race to the holding place:

orange balls fly at my face
and neck and chest:

My aim is off and
a kid takes one to the head:

The balls are soft and don't hurt,

only sting a little,

but they shake it off,
laughter and shrieks frothing around us

as a game erases
frustration:

An alarm clangs, announcing it's time
to return inside and read stories:

We're all disappointed
but we know we'll be back soon enough

because of short tempers
and family togetherness:

Peace doesn't last
long.

So...Back to Orange Juice

It practically glows in a cup,
neon orange against
the green backdrop of my kitchen.

It's been years since I drank it—
too much sugar and too many calories
to fit my health-conscious life.

But every now and then
I cannot pass by the refrigerated section
without grabbing a jug.

When I tip back my head
and let the cold liquid coat my throat,
the taste throws me back a sixteen years,

to the days I would drink a glass
before recording the kick counts
of my first son,

all my senses alive
with ensuring he, too,
was alive.

He would stretch and strike and tumble

as soon as the sugar reached him,
the lines between us

natural, steady, unbreakable.
The lines between us now
are snared, fraying,

blocked and constricted,
forced sometimes.
Many days I ache for the

easy connection that
didn't require prying out of him
a single word.

So I pour another glass of orange juice
and invite him to the table.
Maybe the memory, laid down

before he had the slightest knowledge
of the world and its workings,
will reconnect us,

mother to son.

Yellow

The Yellow Truck

>It was off-limits to us

He took us for a ride in it once
made us sit in the bed
where the stars kept us company

Every now and then we'd find
enough courage to lift our heads
feel the wind blast in our face

squint our eyes to peer into the front
where he had his arm
around our mother

I could always tell
when he was back home
I'd step off the bus

and see him washing and
shining that truck, giving it
the love and attention he could not give us

Once when we were playing hide and seek
I climbed up in the bed and
imagined I could hear him yelling—

because sometimes yelling
was better than silence
when the word silence spoke was

                gone

An Appreciation for the Finer Things

The sun turns the room gold.
My cats recline in the glow
with the same kind of freedom
I'd like to have.
I stretch out.
The warmth slips into my chest,
hope braided through it.
For a moment
the despair was cold,
but the night recedes
in the dappling light.

There is not
a cloud in the sky.

•

We drive to the library.
I forgot my sunglasses,
but I don't squint for long.

•

It's these moments in the sunshine,
feeling the warmth splash my face,

watching the way it gathers
all the colors of the land and
soaks them in life
that I truly know
how marvelous is this
               universe.

Two Snakes

She didn't stop long enough
to see which way those stripes went—
red and yellow, red and black
it didn't matter
                it was a snake

and when she saw it
she waved us to the car
rummaged through the supplies
for a shovel, hacked it to pieces
in her Sunday dress

There were two of them
one eating another
one cleaning the world of
                snakes
but she didn't bother
with details like that
she only saw a
                snake
and her defenses lifted to
meet them like her dress
lifted around her knees

Some things

                        snakes
are worth
the undignified show
of elimination

At Odds

one year I dressed up
as Miss America for Halloween

I wore a yellow dress that
shimmered in the moon glow

and billowed out from my waist
so you couldn't quite tell how thick it was

a crepe sash with the words "Miss America"
in black block letters completed the look

I did not know then how restrictive
a beauty contest could be

I was years away from learning
I was too unattractive

      too disappointing
      too "big-boned"

to even gain entry
but I would know

the world would

make sure of it

and one day I
started skipping lunch

maybe it was the way they looked at me
maybe someone said something

maybe it's what all ten-year-old girls do
when they realize they don't

have what it takes to be Miss America
in a world that demands it

What Playground?

Way back when
seesaws still waited on
elementary school playgrounds

and two kids raced to pick the seat
Way back when
their weight balanced

life hadn't curled
its bony fingers around them yet
choked off their breath

Way back when
before conspiracy theories and
crude jokes

> before hate spilled inkblots
> that stained
> love and trust and hope

Way back when
the seesaws squealed and
made their presence known

But that playground

was torn down
years ago

In Appreciation For National Geographic

My whole body
thrums with excitement
the moment I spy its yellow cover
among the envelopes and fliers
        regular boring old mail

I know the words
contained within it
will broaden my mind
and a broad mind is an open mind
and an open mind is
        a malleable vessel

for listening
    accepting
        loving

I flip open the first page
and begin to
        awaken

White

Report Cards

I brought home report cards
with predictable regularity,
though my mother likely knew
everything I was doing at the school;

she was, after all, the librarian.

I learned early on what report cards
were supposed to look like.
When my father left, I thought
those six-week assessments
were something I could hold out,
> a peace offering
> a lure back home

which is why I graduated with a 106 final average.

He didn't even come
to hear
> my valedictorian speech.

My kids bring home report cards now,
and I'm careful to delineate between
doing their best and

being the best—

it doesn't take much for those white pages
to tell you
        who you are.

Perspective

My father had to wear a white brace
after an accident that broke his neck.
My mother didn't share any of the details with us,
just drove us to the hospital
where he lay hooked up to machines,
a beep counting the beats of his heart.
I learned later he'd been drinking and rolled the car
when he thought
the headlights coming at him
had crossed over into his lane.

It was the first time I saw
my seemingly unbreakable father
broken.

I don't remember how long he wore the brace,
but I do remember how he stood ramrod straight,
how he turned his head ever so slowly,
how he used his eyes
instead of his belt
to speak his displeasure.
He could not exert himself more than the brace would allow,
and so we had the time of our lives.

It was his shackle but
our freedom.

In Concert With Fairies

Her ceiling had sparkles on it,
winking from the rough texture
that looked like a white gravel road
turned upside down above our heads.
It didn't need sunlight to glitter,
only an errant beam from
the table lamp.

She told us the sparkles
were lights in the attic,
from the fairies who lived there.
She told us they watched over
the people who slept in her house.
She told us they had grand parties
and glowed at all hours of the day.

I believed her,
and it made her house seem magical.
My cousins were so lucky to live there.
I'd never had a house with
fairies in the attic.

As soon as I walked in her door,
I would look up at the ceiling
and imagine what those fairies

were doing.
    Dancing?
    Singing?
    Sleeping with
        their glow still brilliant?
I never could find the attic door
to investigate, but I certainly tried.
The magic never diminished.

Even twenty-five years later,
when I walked into her house grown
and with children of my own,
my eyes lifted to the sparkles,
to the holes that led straight to the attic,
to the fairy glow.

Hold the Sugar

Nana loved us with
vanilla, thick cream, and sugar.
She'd pour and shake the ingredients
into a hand-cranked machine,
and it would take an hour or more
to freeze enough so we could eat it
as ice cream instead of sweet milk.
We sat on our hands and waited.

She'd done it so many times
she didn't even have to use measuring cups.
The days we visited her single-wide
the ice cream maker was already
waiting on the counter and
we'd look at each other and grin.
Nana's word—*give them as much as they want*—
was law in her house.
My mother rolled her eyes.

It always came out
perfect: creamy, sweet, rich.

The day she forgot the sugar
and it tasted like frozen cream with salt,
she scolded us for not telling her until

she sat down with a bowl of her own,
wondering why no one else was eating.
We all laughed about her blunder
and entered the story into family legend.
Little did we know it was no laughing matter,
it was the beginning of
the slow decline into the
end.

Her ice cream
would never be the same,
and neither would she.

Home is Where the Walls Are Blue

I could never bear
plain white walls,
though I love simplicity.

Plain white walls
never felt like
home.

For a while,
when I was a kid,
we didn't paint or hang

anything on walls—
our lives were transitory,
and we never knew when

we'd next pick up
and move again,
usually by necessity.

When I bought my first home,
I painted almost every wall
and hung pictures and artwork and mirrors.

I stayed there seventeen years and counting—

longer than I'd lived
anywhere in my life.

Writing Cramp

sometimes the
white page of a notebook feels
like an opportunity

where lines wait for recording
where thoughts have space to accumulate
where a brand-new or ancient idea can arrange itself

    in an innovative way

and sometimes it feels
like an accusation
like a confirmation of novice

like the years invested in writing mean
absolutely nothing
to this

        blank white page

and as I open my notebook
I wonder which it will be
today

The Picture of Us

Every Easter,
when I was a child,
my great-grandmother would make
my sister and me matching dresses.
My mother would coordinate
her new dress with ours.
She would place an Easter hat
on our heads, spin us around,
and I'd gaze in the mirror and think
I looked just like a Southern belle.
We'd stand closer together
for a family picture,
sometimes five of us,
when my dad was home,
sometimes only four.

The last picture we took
was one in which my brother wore a tie,
my sister and I wore white hats,
my mother wore a flower in her hair
and my father wore a white neck brace
from a car accident that happened
after a visit to a bar.

When I look at that picture today,

it tells nothing of what
simmered underneath.
In the eyes of the family smiling back,
there is no hint of
      the infidelity
      the scars
      the trauma

           the words
           no amount of time
           can erase.

First Home

we hung pictures
all over the white walls

tried to tell our stories with
sunbursts and perfectly symmetrical rectangles

and collages scribbled
with poetry

when we left that place
we had to fill in dozens of holes

we never hung
those pictures again

There is No Miracle

They tell me
what's in the bottle
will keep me looking young,

but every time
I glance in the mirror,
I see another wrinkle.

No miracle cream
stops the marks of
time.

In Response to the Question "Why Are There Notecards in Your Purse?"

The notecards capture my ideas
every thought that could
become more than a thought
every wondering
every interesting word

They become my muse

A Wedding Can Save You, Too

It was the perfect princess dress

It hung a little off the shoulders
and billowed out into an A-line
and had tiny pink flowers
that sparkled when I turned
a certain way
It was beautiful
and I knew it was the one
as soon as I saw it

In this dress
I would walk down an aisle
promise my everlasting love
pose for pictures
       dance
              eat
       socialize
and at the end of the evening
my new husband would peel it off
and it would remain
           all the years after
in a case shoved in
the back of my closet
a memory of the night

I played princess
and saved myself

Red

The Razing of the Red Roof

The elementary school
was a red-roofed building with a
pier-and-beam foundation that
made the floor bow and groan when you walked.
Inside was a room off the auditorium
that everyone said was haunted.
I only entered that room once,
when my teacher beckoned me
up some stairs and into a candlelit space
where she traced my profile onto a piece of black paper
that would later be cut out and framed
and given to my mother.
She would hang it on the wall
of our home for a time,
and then it would move to the closet,
along with the profiles of
my brother and sister.

It was the place my mother
would send us when she needed a break
and we needed to swing and
race down a metal slide and
spin on a merry-go-round.
It was the place where my friend
knocked out a tooth coming down

the slide head-first,
where my brother choked on
a chicken bone in the cafeteria,
where a boy smashed a spider on a sidewalk
and thousands of babies on its back scattered,
inducing nightmares for weeks.
It was the place where
I fell in love with reading,
where I discovered I needed glasses,
where I developed my first crush
as he moonwalked across the auditorium stage
just like Michael Jackson.

It was the place where
I learned about training bras, periods,
and what it meant to become a woman.

They tore down
that red-roofed elementary school,
and when they did,
it felt like they tore down
a part of me, too.

The Color of Death

She had every color of the rainbow
in that Tupperware collection.
But the one she used most often
was the square one with rounded edges
and a starburst lid.

She put Hamburger Helper in it.
Sometimes it tasted green beans or spaghetti.
Other times it held a bunch of grapes.
You never knew what you were going to get
when you opened that red container in her refrigerator.
But one thing was for certain:
It was always there.

Until the day it wasn't.

The Folders are Everywhere For Now

For as long as I can remember
we've had red folders
littering out countertops.
In kindergarten they are behavior folders,
sent home to let parents know
what their kids did wrong today.
In first grade they're for communication
and homework that will elicit endless complaints.
In second grade they carry
completed work home, grades attached.
The purpose of those folders becomes
a little vague the older my sons get—
all I know is they speak of routine, of delight,
of humorous memories we'll laugh about later.
("Do you know how many times
your older brother brought a note
home from his teacher?" I told
my devastated third son the other day.)
They offer a glimpse of personality,
a chance at connection,
an opportunity to save
something special.

And though sometimes it annoys me
to see them stacked up and spread out,

I will surely miss them
when they're gone,
another artifact lost to time.

Don't Think About the Things That Can Happen on a Greyhound Bus

My sister and I visited
my father on spring break
my junior year of college—
rode the whole way to The Sunshine State
on a Greyhound bus,
two young girls traveling alone,
pushed to the center aisle because
men wouldn't give up their seats
They watched us the entire trip
and did not try to hide it

My luggage was lost somewhere
between Alabama and Texas,
went all the way to Memphis
or somewhere north instead of
down south to Florida
It returned to me two days later,
only because of the persistence
of my stepmother

We hadn't seen my father
in almost ten years

My stepmother bought

a whole case of strawberries,
ten pounds of them, grown fresh
in a neighboring town
My sister and I ate them
until we were sick,
those beautiful red berries
sticking to our fingers,
turning heavy in our stomachs

When it was time to leave,
we told our father we
did not want to return by bus
He saw the determination in our eyes,
or maybe he knew the things that could
happen to young girls alone on a Greyhound bus
and for once in his life he made the right decision
and drove us halfway home,
my mother closing the distance

My memories of that trip
are tinged with red, but it is not
the strawberries I see when I look back,
it is the fear that pulsed behind my eyes
the fear of being a young, beautiful,
desirable woman became a
red-hot, dangerous thing

Betrayal is Not Such a Good Friend After All

Betrayal traveled to Houston with me
to help pick out my wedding dress,
ate lunch with my family and friends,
drove all the way back.
We had a good,
stimulating conversation
while maybe she planned
how she would take me
down.

Betrayal spread lies
and claimed them as truth,
wedged herself between me and a future,
gave me a choice I didn't want
to make: her or him.

Betrayal did not show up
at my wedding
but left that red dress
to gather dust in a closet.

The Colors We Claim

Red was my power color.
I reached for it when I needed confidence—
    a job interview,
    an important concert,
    a first date with my future husband.

Red found me at the bottom,
dusted me off,
told me I was more than a girl
waiting on a call from her father,
wondering what she'd done wrong,
wishing she could be what he wanted.

Red reminded me
who I could be:
    Powerful,
    strong,
    loved.

There's No Place Like Home

I knew I was home
when I saw the
strawberries.

When I stayed with my Memaw
for a week in the summer
I returned home to a kitchen
full of pots painted with
strawberries.

When I shipped off to drum major camp,
my first extended stay away from my mother,
away from all my family,
I closed my eyes and imagined
the strawberry towels that hung
beside the kitchen window,
and soon enough I was back
home.

The summer I spent a week
with my dad and his new family,
I ached for the strawberry cookie jar
that never had any cookies in it
because Mom thought they
turned stale in cookie jars,

and the days did not pass faster,
but they at least passed remembering
home.

When I left for college,
those strawberry shards of life
populated my dreams,
coloring them red and large and
sweet.

When I visit my mother now,
though I've not lived in
that house for eighteen years,
the strawberries still
reach through memories
with one word:
Home.

The Red Pen of Correction

When I was in third grade,
my teacher let me write in pen
because I had good handwriting
and I always took care with my words.
She didn't realize the privilege of
using a pen played into my
perfectionistic tendencies—
so long as you didn't make
too many mistakes, you got to
keep using a pen.
I made no mistakes.

It was only later that I came to know,
with no small sense of consternation,
a different kind of pen:
didn't write this in a complete sentence,
my fourth-grade teacher scrawled on one assignment,
added several unnecessary steps to this proof,
my ninth grade geometry teacher wrote on another,
probably not much of a future for you here,
wrote my creative writing professor in college,
on the back of one of my
(probably somewhat melodramatic)
poems.

I hated that pen because it
shattered my illusion of perfect,
which undermined the simplicity
of being good enough.
Every time that pen came out,
I felt a little smaller than
I had before.

But eventually
I came to see it
for what it really was:
an opportunity to improve.

Red became an open door.

Black

Resolutions of the Young

    On the blacktop
we learned how to dribble
stopped to watch them play
on our way back home
dreamed about what it would be like
to slam dunk

    On the blacktop
we whispered about boys
behind cupped hands
predicted which one would be
the victor on the court
which in our minds made him
better than all the others
potential boyfriend material even
we were still too young to imagine
anything beyond kissing or holding hands
or love notes left on desks

    On the blacktop
I once hit a girl for
making fun of my brother
once ducked away before
anyone could point fingers at me
once felt the blaze of shame for

what I'd done and what we were—
just another broke white family
on the wrong side of the tracks

    On the blacktop
I decided I wanted
to be more

You May Wonder What Shoes Can Do

if I want to feel

> taller
> more desirable
> more powerful

I slip on my black heels

Should We Tell What Happens on Playgrounds?

they creaked in the wind
as though complaining to the children
of their loneliness

and so the children filled them
pumped their legs
stretched their toes up to the sky

and the chains still rattled
and the swings still moaned
but it was a happy sound now

full and alive and useful
because they served
their purpose

and then one day
just beside the seesaws
he made her play truth or dare

made her choose dare
made her expose herself in exchange
for his own exposing

they were
only
children

she walked home in shame
as the swings creaked in the background
no longer full and alive and useful

only used

The Unknowable Cannot Stop Her

Light splashes across sidewalks
edges swallowed by darkness
shadows bend and waver

she can't see what
lies beyond but even so
she steps out

into the unknown
is far better than
stagnation

Let the Music Play

the notes across the page
did not feel foreign
even if it was the
first time I saw them

they fell into place
     a story
and my fingers moved as though
carried by a force that was
not entirely my own but was
made of love and hope and truth

I practiced over and over and over again
mastering my instrument
but also
     in the fading of my world
mastering   abandonment
               abuse
               addiction

the notes were black
but they washed the world

clear

The Things You Can Be on a Trampoline

i
out back is a trampoline
that entertains them for
hours of the day

they squeal kick jump laugh

they deepen their bond as brothers
jumping their way into a
richer understanding of life

ii
when I was a kid
I wanted a trampoline
the girl who lived next door
on our country road
had one and
sometimes she would
invite us over to jump

but the first time her mother
ran screaming from the house
pelting us with unmentionable words
we never went back

iii
for snuggle time one evening
my son asked me to jump
with him on our trampoline
I hadn't done it since I was a kid
but how hard could it be
I would have fun
he would have fun
the night would be a success

we jumped for fifteen minutes
his giggle piercing
    the quiet of the world
my muscles piercing
    the quiet of my thoughts

after
    fifteen years and
    six kids
it's not the same at all

iv
I used to imagine I could
be anything on the trampoline—
    someone who could fly
    an astronaut
    a cheerleader even—

        the air splits were easier
        when you attempted them
        on a springy surface

but when my feet touched
the ground again
my love affair with gravity ended
and I was just the same
    old
        me

v
my sons imagine
they can be anyone
and do anything

I will let them believe it
as long as they can
out there on a trampoline

that might bounce them
high enough to touch the sky
or maybe just touch each other

a ring of brothers
on the same journey forward
into the unknown

Philosophical Wonderings

I don't know why I chose it.
Black and silver were favorite colors,
but that seems too superficial.
I like to think the band director
looked at my fingers and said,
She'd make a good clarinet player,
as though physical features had
anything to do with excellence.
But the details escape me.
I came home that day of band class
with a clarinet.

It was my first real instrument,
not counting the piano with which
I'd tinkered when I was younger
and had no desire to practice.
But now I had a clarinet
and a father who'd left
and an urge to prove
I could be somebody.

Excelling at an instrument was,
        to me,
very much like disciplining
my body to eat less food

as I spiraled into anorexia:
I could control it.
I set my metronome,
      set my timer,
           warmed up with scales,
     focusing on the ones that
gave me trouble,
      then practiced my musical
           pieces systematically,
     slowing the metronome through
difficult fingerings to first get
the rhythm and notes perfected,
then speeding up as my
proficiency increased.
Every part of it was
      planned,
           controlled,
                efficient.
When I played the music,
the world drifted away,
but the pursuit of excellence
always clung to the edges.
I practiced so I could be excellent,
so I could rise above the rest,
so I could,
         in losing myself,
win.

Did I ever really
love the clarinet,
or was it merely a way
to defy my invisibility and
be seen?

Back in the Mustang Days

For a while he didn't have a car,
rode his bike
> to meet me for dates,
> to work,
> to the grocery store,
>> bags balanced on handlebars.

Then he bought
a sexy black Mustang,
> vintage,
> fast,
> cheap,

that looked like its paint
belonged to a bass boat,
> sparkles included.

He got more tickets in that car
than any other, perhaps
a case study in profiling.
It didn't bother him much;
he was never in any real danger.
The driver's seat sat crooked
so on long trips his back knotted up,
needed stretching upon
arrival at the destination.
The air conditioner didn't work,

so we rolled down the windows
and let it toss our hair
in every direction.

We held hands across the stick shift,
flew down highways,
laughed about our futures
       in that car,
so when it came time to sell it
we almost couldn't let it go.
Like most first cars
bought without a parent's help
upon moving out of their house,
it was a testament to
       hard work,
              miraculous savings,
                     and sheer stupidity.

Chance

The post office sat a few blocks
from our house, and Mom
would walk there alone most days,
probably for a little time to herself.
But one day she took us all,
even our spotted dog Chance.

To get to the post office in our tiny town,
>   which had only a phone company,
>   a volunteer fire department,
>   and a mercantile with one gas pump
>   that would close down in later years,

you had to cross Highway 111.
It wasn't always dangerous;
this was small-town Texas,
and the speed limit lowered
to a crawl in the town. Some people
wanted to beat the train, though,
and they'd race toward the tracks,
oblivious to any waiting to cross the road.
I only mention that because
I observed it once or twice,
not because that's what happened
this particular day.

I'm not really sure what happened
this particular day.
Maybe Chance saw something
he wanted to chase.
Maybe it was a car and
I just don't remember that
he liked to chase cars.
Maybe he simply ran ahead of us
because he knew where we were going
and wanted to lead the way.

I do remember
       the brakes on that car squealing,
       the awful yelp of our dog,
       the way Chance spun in the middle of the road
              limbs splayed out and whirling
              like the blades of a windmill.

It only took him a minute to
shake off the stun and get back up
and return to us, limping a little
but tail wagging, his name
ringing out like a prophecy.
In the end, the only thing that remained
to remind us of that accident
were the four black lines,
where rubber had burned onto the road

in a driver's desperation to stop.

Here Kitty

They move in the shadows of the night
    a streak across your path
    so you question whether
    you've seen one at all
        until their eyes catch light
        and turn them other-worldly
a ghostly spirit
a haunting creature

        a curse to see one, folklore says

At the adoption center
when my sons took the black cat
out of her enclosure
the animal rights activist said
not many adopt black cats
My sons asked why
She said because people believe
    they're bad luck

As advanced as
our culture has become
    it is still primitive

We took the black cat home

and named her
                Brook

There You Go Messing With the Sacred

                black on white
is a solace
I sought them when
the tension in my house
stretched too tight
when the letter showed up
in our mail and explained
his absence by revealing
The Replacements
when the accusations
and wonderings battered
my heart into a pulp
fiction only could stanch

                black on white
is a remembrance
in the pages I met
the people who had held
this book in their hands,
read the words
recorded in minds or notebooks
what was profound and worth
storing away for
a later time

        black on white
is a freedom
from the trappings of the world
the son across the room asking
if he can have a snack
the permission slip on the counter
awaiting three dollar bills
I'll have to take a trip
to the bank to get
the supper boiling
on the stove

one day I pick up the iPad
to read an ebook
aloud to my kids,
and he's changed the
reading settings to
a black screen with white words
and I tell myself it's just preference
it's not because those pages
aren't as sacred to him
as they are to me
this is only a
simple misunderstanding
how can he know
the importance of
        black on white

if I have never told him
how can anyone know
another person fully

but I wonder still:

                black on white
am I as known
as I thought I was?

When Night Came Stalking

    At night
I sat on the porch
looking at the stars
wondering how life could
sometimes look so ugly
when there was so much beauty
in it

    At night
I heard my mother
preparing her
       bags
       books
       clothes
for another day
and I felt safe

    At night
I opened a book
and tried to lose myself
in other worlds

    At night
I listened to my sister breathe
in the bed beside me

and prayed she would be
okay

    At night
I raced through the house
on my way to bed
imagining monsters—
        overly large wolves
        Candyman
        vampires—
chasing me

    At night
I tried to forget
all a day had done to tell me
I was not worthy of such words as
        intelligent
        beautiful
        good enough
        loved

    At night
I could not shut down
my brain and its constant
consideration of the future
in a spiral that didn't
always land on

       goodness
       hope
       redemption

   At night
I lay awake wondering
where he was
what he was doing
whether he ever thought of us

   At night
the words of my father swarmed
     blending with the words of others
circled me like the winds of a tornado
       tangling
       ripping
       shrieking
so I didn't know which was whose
and I certainly couldn't hear my own

   At night
I looked out my window
     into the dark
and I found peace in
the hazy glow of the moon
that seemed to say
     no darkness

is absolute

Blue

This is Why I Prefer Stretchy Pants

scrunch, wriggle
twist, pull
they probably shrank in the wash—consolation

lie down on your back—that makes it easier
stretch stretch stretch
they'll relax as you wear them—justification

suck in hard
fasten
maybe it's time for a change—provocation

breathe

the battle begins
       and ends
with a button—consternation

The False Conundrum

In the beginning, he said,
there were two types of reporters:
those who used black ink,
those who used blue.
He leaned close, coffee breath
wafting across the table.
Which are you?

I thought long and hard
about which to choose—
> on the one hand,
> I prefer black ink,
> but does that make me
>> boring, macabre?
>
> Maybe I should claim blue ink,
> but did it communicate less
>> professionalism,
>
> too much playfulness
> for a beat reporter?

Blue or black?

Well? he said.

I could say something profound,

    like it depends on the day,
    my mood,
    you know—
        but did that sound ridiculous?

What did this situation require?

Blue or black
Blue or black
Blue or black

Black, I blurted,
watching his face for a sign
that I'd chosen wrong,
wondering if it was
too late to retract.
A smile spread across his face.

The good news is, he said,
*you'll always be able to find
a pen in the storage closet.*

And the bad news?

He shrugged.
*It's a necessary question.
For supply needs.*

It wasn't the first time
I over-thought something with
a simple purpose.

Hunter Hunting

It was his eyes
that drew me in

He sat in a church
pretended to be spiritual
but instead had an eye out
for every cute girl who walked in
or maybe he just looked for
the naive ones

He invited me over to his place
I thought what's the harm
he was

>cute
>blonde
>had those piercing blue eyes

I brought a friend
he wasn't too happy about that
but he had a roommate
so he left her with him
pulled me into his bedroom
said he wanted to show me
a song on his guitar

I was a sucker for music—
or maybe I was just naive

he closed the door
>said don't you think two people
>should find out if they're
>sexually compatible before
>they get married?

shoved me on the bed
>(didn't wait for an answer
>or didn't want to hear it)

climbed on top
I somehow scrambled free
he wasn't a large guy
or maybe there is an
unexplainable power that
overtakes a woman pinned down
when pinned down by a
skinny desperate boy

>I ran

my friend beside me
out into the night in
clunky platform shoes
I lost them somewhere along the way
>or maybe I didn't

memory's a foggy thing

I dreamed about those cold
hungry blue eyes looming over me
for months
knowing they would be back
      on another's face
      in another color or shade
but always out there

waiting

The Color of Belief

I don't know if it was
the first piece of home
I unfolded inside my dorm room,
but I do remember it being
the most visible.

I don't remember why I chose blue—
maybe it was my favorite color then,
maybe I'd read in a magazine that
blue was a calming color
and I knew my anxieties
would need calming,
maybe blue moved me
for an entirely different reason.
My imagination likes to construct
the details missing from memory.

The blue was the first thing you'd notice
walking through my dorm room door.

It was the very opposite of her.

•

At family gatherings she was quiet,

kept to the back, watched all the
movement and activity like
she had no need to do anything
but observe.
She laughed easily but discreetly.
The only time I really saw her
steal the light was when
she argued an opinion with
one of my uncles or when the
Trivial Pursuit board came out.
Maybe those light-filled memories
are the construct of my much younger,
more innocent mind.
All I know is she was
the first person who said college
like it was meant
for me.

•

She bought
     my blue comforter,
     my white pillow,
     the beige case that went over it.

She added
     a toaster oven,

      a variety pack of granola bars,
           nourishment on which
           I'd live that first semester
           (and little else),
   and a fifty-dollar bill.

She didn't drop me off at college
like my mom and stepdad did,
but she sent me with a letter.
I hung it on the cork board
above my desk.

The words of that letter
are lost to me today,
but I think what she mostly said
was that she believed in me.

•

No one in my family
had graduated college.
It wasn't what we did.
A couple of them
dropped out a year or two in,
most didn't go at all.
We were the working class.
We had kids to support,

money to make.

I wanted to be a writer.
People like me weren't
supposed to be writers.
We weren't supposed to go to college
or get degrees or secure a job
at a major newspaper
right after graduation.

My first semester of college
I wasn't sure I'd make it.
I'd never been so far from home,
so long away from my mother.
There were nights,
      months of them,
when I wondered if it would just be easier
to go on home and do
what we'd always done:
                work.

But something about that blue comforter,
its connection to her,
the courage it spoke about
what I was made to do
kept me from giving up,
kept me imagining a better

future for myself.

I couldn't let her down.

•

Memaw died eleven years ago.
The only one of my sons
she got to meet was my firstborn.
I have a picture of her, holding him.
They're both grinning at me.
I think of her often—
    what would she say about
        the full house I have,
    what would she think of
        all this writing,
    how would she react to this
        poem about her?

Sometimes I imagine
her small warm hand in mine,
her eyes whispering what
her mouth didn't need to say:

        I always knew you would do it.

Choices

For some of them
I worked on those blankets
while they kicked and stretched and
turned in the womb
rested the fibers against
my swelling belly on trips
or whenever I had a spare moment
which seemed more frequent in the beginning
or maybe that is only
the perception that time gives
when looking back
before priorities shifted

For others
I worked
while their tiny forms
lay strapped to my chest
their faces turned up to mine
so every now and then I could
    glance down
    kiss a pursed mouth
    watch the eyelids flutter
    wonder what sorts of things infants dream

For the last one

I never finished that
crocheted blanket
because every time I had
a spare moment it was only
the smallest fraction of time
                hours
                minutes
                seconds
contracted and shrank
and by the time it widened again
I decided I'd had enough of clacking metal
I'd stitch in my presence
                instead

And so there is no blanket
of this particular sort
for the last son
there are instead
large moments of wonder-filled
                play

Two Tales of Blue

1.
The first thing I noticed
were his eyes—
> so blue they were startling

The girls whispered about him
behind cupped hands
I pretended I didn't notice
he asked me out
I tried not to think it was
more than it was

he was my first kiss
my first serious boyfriend
my first love
but the night he
> pulled me into a room
> took what he wanted
> didn't bother to ask me if
> > it's what I wanted

I left without saying goodbye
and thought

> > good riddance

2.
The first thing I noticed
were his eyes—
        somewhere between blue and green
they changed by the day
and his mood

The girls gossiped about
the songs he wrote
tried to predict which one of us
he'd written them for
he asked me out
I tried not to think it was
more than it was

he was my last kiss
my last serious boyfriend
my last love
and the night he
pulled me onto a stage
        at The Majestic Theatre
        after a ballet performance of *The Nutcracker*
    knelt in front of me
    and asked me to marry him
I stayed and said
yes to
            forever

The Perfect Fit

I pushed pulled twisted turned
but no matter how I
contorted my body
I could not get those jeans
over my ass
They must have shrunk
in the wash, I said
and tossed them aside
      reached for another.

They must have shrunk too.

•

      Six months later
I pulled on those jeans
without unbuttoning them
they were so loose
I wondered if I'd wandered
into the wrong closet
      but no
they were mine
swallowing me
          whole

•

The marriage hung tight around me
we rarely did anything
without the other
mostly I went where he went
    wasn't that what wives
    were supposed to do
I took his name and somehow
    forgot my own
by the time I remembered
I could scarcely breathe around
    the choker
of expectation

•

Sixteen years later
I'd grown so small
you could see the
unintended open spaces
    those places where
    condemnation crept in like
    midnight shadows
        breathing guilt
        around words like

you should be better
you should apologize
you should be grateful he's still around
you should be ashamed of yourself

        you should be more

•

They say
      nothing
ever really fits
the way you want it to
maybe they're right

It Says a Lot About Me, I Guess

>You need the right socks, she said,
>ones that wick the moisture

as if I don't know how much feet sweat
on an eight-mile run
as if I don't know how they smell
after all morning trapped in a running shoe
as if I've never looked at the choices
and wondered if it's all just a mind game
>this promise to absorb odor and sweat

because I spent more money
on a pair of socks than on
my running pants and
my feet are still damp and foul
when I remove my shoes

False advertising for these blue socks
or do I simply have exceptionally
stubborn feet?

Resolution

Sometimes I stop and stare
and think I don't look in his eyes

often enough
I don't always see

the blue that turns to green
and the emotions that hide inside

I don't always pay attention
to his existence because

he is self sufficient and
life is busy

and so many other voices
shout for my attention

but the other day
I noticed

his long legs
his sharpening jaw

the way time

has stretched and shaped him

and I told myself
I will look into his soul

at least once a day
so I can see him

before he grows up and
leaves

Into the Blue

You know you've reached
the apex of not liking yourself
when you opt for blue-colored contact lenses
to turn your boring brown eyes
more arresting
It's subjective, really
Your definition
Everything's brown,
like you were born in a sepia world—
eyes, hair, even your skin
looks pale brown in certain lights
A little color would be good for you

All they really do is
wash out your complexion,
make you look sickly all the time
You weren't born with blue eyes,
and it shows

One day you'll look back
at those pictures snapped
your senior year of high school
and wonder why you loved
everyone but yourself

Purple

What I See When I Think of Her

she wore them every evening
and almost all day on weekends

when she left the house
they waited by her bedroom door
like faithful puppies

and when she was gone
the hardest things to walk past
without breaking

were those
purple slippers

The Story in a Dress

We wore purple to his wedding
    stood in a sunlit room
        snapped photos with the rays
        illuminating our backs

We smiled
    laughed
        toasted them into
        family

but the hits took their toll
    piled up
        bowed them over like
        young oaks in a hurricane

and the storm skies
never cleared

Ten years later
that purple dress still
hangs in my closet
        six sizes too big
but it outlasted
love

Good Riddance

They sagged and sank
bowed a little in the middle
so when you sat next to
someone you liked
        maybe even loved
the spent cushions drew you closer
It was especially inconvenient
when sitting next to
the former best friend
who would make a valiant attempt
to crumple up my reputation
I didn't like her
I certainly didn't love her

They lasted longer
than they perhaps should have
draped in purple-striped
couch covers

But when I married
I left them out by a dumpster
too many unpleasant memories
clinging to fibers to even consider
artfully arranging them for pickup
on the side of a country road

A Note to Marketing Professionals

If you want my money
all you have to do
is make something in
purple

The Dress that Began the Dance

one year I dressed up for Halloween
        wriggled into a medieval dress
        in my favorite shade of purple

I thought I looked quite good
        regal even
but a picture snapped unawares told the truth

the next year I wore the same dress
it hung from me
like an oversized blanket

because sometimes pictures
show you what you don't want
to see and next thing you know

you're dancing with
        an eating disorder and
no one knows it's time to cut in

So Special

I got it for Christmas one year,
and it was the only thing
I'd write with for weeks,
switching between red and green
and blue and orange.
I carried it everywhere,
not bothering with pockets and purses,
where it could get lost,
but holding it tight.
If anyone wanted to use it,
I'd decline,

>*no, sorry,*
>
>*it's my special pen.*

I thought it had to be the most
wonderful invention in the world—
at least until I returned to school
and Shelly Billstein carried around
a ten-color pen that included
my favorite shade: purple.

It doesn't take long for
>*enough*

to become

>*more more more*

Sometimes You Can Touch the Invisible

we stood beneath
the grand arches of a castle
           in purple

while they pledged their love
and the sun went down

it was a perfect ceremony
ringed
           in purple

but maybe nothing lasts forever
as they say

and now
all that's left to see
           in purple

are hearts that stood, too
beating

Missing

You could always tell
which glass was hers

she didn't use a straw
so the lip always had

a ring of her
purple lipstick

It's strange,
the little things that become

a giant ache in our chest
once a person is gone

I have searched
a thousand glasses,

but I have never found one
with her stain on it

Favorite is Flexible

The back door slams. *I picked this for you*, he says, thrusting a flower in my lap, where it slides into the middle seam of my notebook.

Thank you. I pick it up and smell it, delicate purple petals rippling in the fan's barely-there breeze.

It's your favorite color, he says, certain, matter-of-fact.

I agree.

Put it in some water, he says.

I don't always fancy getting orders from four-year-olds, but you have to understand: this one's cute.

I do what he says, watch the flower float on top of the water like a lily pad.

I should get some more, he says.

I don't disagree.

But only purple! He races out the door.

Even if purple wasn't my favorite color, it is now.

Preferences
and favorites bow to the whims
of a darling child

When You Know, You Know

On our first date
he showed up with

> a bouquet of purple flowers
> a guitar strapped on his back
> an invitation to see the sunrise
> > from a mountain

The sky hung heavy that day,
no sun rewarding our breathless climb,

but we made music all the same,
and by the time those purple flowers

wilted in their vase
I knew we'd last forever

Once Upon a Morning

it happened in a split second
my toe caught on a tiny lip
maybe it wasn't even a lip
I've run that same sidewalk
a hundred times

but isn't that just like
the unexpected,
reaching out to trip
the unaware

I didn't have time
to catch myself

and isn't that just like life,
leaving little time for
bracing against what might
kill (or destroy) us

you can tell it from my injuries—
busted knee
a wrist that looks like
it fought asphalt
a scabbed elbow
but that's nothing to the

bruised breastbone that
makes it hurt to breathe

and isn't that just the way
injuries go
it's the ones you can't see
that hurt the worst
that make you wonder
if you'll even be able
to peel yourself out of bed
much less
      walk

            run

                  live

I Can See Myself

On the way home
from a doctor's appointment
I saw a purple marker
clinging to the back
of a Honda Pilot.

We turned left
      the marker held on
we turned right
      the marker held on.
We went round bend after bend and
      the marker held on.

How long would it
hold on?

On the way home
from a doctor's appointment
I saw a purple marker
clinging to the back
of a Honda Pilot.

It did not roll off the edge
and I knew then that neither
would I.

Brown

A House of Pecans

Here is the house:
wide
stone-faced
still

Here are the trees:
canopied shade throwing
shadows over the
backyard

Here are the pecans:
crackling underfoot

Here is the memory:
racing to collect
as many as we could
dodge the tire swing
dodge the nuts at our feet
dodge the man who was back home
for who knew how long
a reign of terror as
wide and
stone-faced and
still as the house

Sorry Not Sorry

In the style of William Carlos Williams' "This is Just to Say"

This is just to say
I have eaten the tater tots
That sat on
Your plate

And which
You were likely
Planning
For your indulgent snack

Forgive me
They were magnificent
So crisp
So salty

Mud Can Be a Friend or a Monster

i

It speckles the back of
my running shoes,
a testament to the miles
and mind-wandering and
the mercies of silence,
mornings spent
pounding pavement,
settling into a pace,
running as far away from home
as I possibly can
before the tethers
pull me back

ii

After a morning outside,
they track it in,
footprints that reveal
their paths to
          books,
    food,
Legos.

iii

Once when I was a teenager
my brother and I found
a pit beside our house
We were too old for such things,
but we flung wet earth at one another,
laughter ringing out
into an evening sky
We rinsed off with a hose,
but our mother still saw
the damning evidence,
as mothers do

iv

At three years old
I tried to jump over a ditch
that was too wide for me
I fell in,
sullied a brand-new
birthday outfit
and emerged looking
like a bog monster

v

I don't mind
the rain so much

I quite enjoy the smell of wet yards
and watching the rivulets
settle into cracks

Just leave the muddy shoes
at the door

Copper Consolation

The first words
he said about the divorce:
> *Well, kids, shit happens.*

> *There's your room—*
the words he said when
he pointed to the tent
> three hundred meters
from the comfortable camper
he shared with his new family.

> *Divide it up:*
the words he tossed back
over his shoulder as he
headed to the camper and
the ones who'd won his heart.

We stared at the
giant Ozarka container
full of copper pennies.
It looked like an impressive
consolation prize for becoming
> The Replaced,
at least until we did what he said.
> Twenty three dollars

is all we were worth that summer.

What Lies Beneath

It was the kind of carpet
that reminded you of dirt

no telling what
hid in its fibers

the carpet had been there
at least half a century

gathering dust and the dead cells
of other people

but she plastered on that smile
ran the vacuum in twenty-five passes

and said, *The furniture
will cover most of it*

the broke learn to live
with what they get

Once Upon a Start

We spent the first days
of our marriage in
a magical place:
Disney World.
I don't remember what we wore,
only the packets of
lingerie I brought
(the only time I really wore it).
Pictures of him show a tan shirt
with a palm tree I'd picked out
during one of my honeymoon clothes
buying sprees.
He wore it twice,
his eyes bright and young,

and every time he pulled it on
        one thousand miles
                seven plus years away
from the magical start,
I remembered
                fun
                connection
                hope.

Two years ago

he pulled out that shirt.
It didn't fit anymore.
Should I get rid of it? he said.

I almost said no.
But we were simplifying.
What was the point of keeping
something that
didn't fit?

He tossed it out.
Now the shirt lives
only in photographs.

And memories.

Tots

In college
I steered clear of
    pizza
    burgers
    chips and queso
by convincing myself
I did not like them
they made me sick
I would not enjoy even the tiniest taste

For some reason
I could never do it with
tater tots

Crisp
salty
greasy
cylindrical inch of
perfection

Sweetening the Deal

When I was young
my grandmother used to pay
my brother and sister and me
to collect pecans for her pies.
We'd race through the yard
gathering buckets in exchange for
a dollar and a slice of
gooey caramelized sugar
with perfectly placed pecans
browned on top,
flaky crust melting under
the weight and stretch of corn syrup.
Her eyes would shine with pleasure
when we asked for
one more piece.

Get me more pecans, she'd say,
and I'll make another.

We'd gather until the sun
dipped low in the sky.
She'd hand us a bowl to shell,
woody oval cracking between
the arms of a metal contraption,
halves springing open to

show the meaty inside.
Sometimes all that effort really did
was put another pecan in our belly,
but she always had enough pieces
to satisfy the sweet teeth of
grandchildren, sons and daughters,
the quiet man who had her heart.

Two pecan trees in our backyard
sometimes offer us their bounty.
I don't pay my sons to collect
those meager offerings, but
on the rare day they find
pecans on the ground,
they carry them inside,
excitement teetering their voices,
to crack between the same
metal contraption.
We share the nutty flesh
and I remember those happy
years of gathering, exchanging,
partaking in the sweetness
expert hands can make
out of droppings left in
the dust.

A Meditation on the Infinite

They used to file back inside,
dirt ringing their lips as though
they'd made mud pies that
tasted too good
to forgo one little lick,
which became
       fingerfuls,
              fistfuls,
                     mouthfuls.

Have you been eating dirt?

No! they'd insist,
that telltale ring of brown
telling the real truth.

•

We haven't planted
a garden in years.
I miss the tilling of the earth,
the transformation of
our backyard into
a colorful paradise of
       tomatoes

           cucumbers
      squash
          berries
      lemons
          limes.

Today I hand
one of my sons
a pot in which
I planted a lemon seed.
This is your lemon tree, I tell him.
Tend it well.

A garden must start
somewhere.

•

If I wish to see where
their feet have carried them,
the places they most often visit,
I have only to observe
the worn paths in our yard,
grass trodden away,
dirt waving through.

•

When I was a teenager,
I used to watch
the dust tornadoes
kicked up by the wind
in the corn field across
the street from my house.
They weren't dangerous
or even frightening,
just earth playing.

Sometimes when it rained,
the precipitation was so dirty
it left mud spots on our
      cars
            porches
     shirts
if we forgot our umbrella.

This morning, when I
walked out to my car
and saw last night's dirty rain
      an anomaly where I live now
spotting it,
a strange sadness
stole over me.

I miss my mom
and pre-quarantine life.

•

Later I take off my shoes,
step into the backyard,
close my eyes and
feel the earth hum
beneath my soles.

What a beautiful thing,
to know that you are alive,
to recognize a day
full of wild possibility,
to remember that though
we return to dust
we live on in a million
different ways.

We are infinite.

The End

About the Author

Rachel Toalson is the award-winning author of nine poetry books, including *this is how you know*, *Life: a definition of terms*, *The Book of Uncommon Hours*, *Textbook of an Ordinary Life*, *this is how you live*, *Sincerely Yours*, *Textbook of a Parenthetical Life*, *Textbook of an Extraordinary Life*; and *this is how you fly*; several middle grade and young adult books; and multiple essay collections as well as books for children under a pen name. She has been writing poetry since the time she could hold a pencil and form letters into words. Her first introduction to poetry was the brilliance of Shel Silverstein, whom she still reads with great pleasure today.

Her poems for children and adults can be read in literary magazines and online publications around the world.

Rachel lives with her husband and six children in San Antonio, Texas.

Author's Note

My dear reader,

It takes every color to make a life.

And even the most undesirable colors (brown? Who says, "My favorite color is brown," besides my husband—because it's the color of my eyes?) have both beautiful and not-so-beautiful memories and experiences associated with them. But what is joy without challenge? How do we truly feel happiness without a little bit of despondency? The difficult memories make the wonderful a little more brilliant. We see that in looking back.

At least I've seen that in looking back. I hope you have, too.

As you go about your "one magnificent life," I hope you start to pay a little more attention to the colors infusing your day. Do you notice the neon pink and orange of the sunrise? The white glow of the moon? The deep green of the tree out back, refreshed by a recent rain?

I hope you live the colors of your life to the fullest. Be brilliant and neon and bright.

In love,
Rachel

P.S. Please don't forget to leave a review and share this book with your friends. Reviews help other readers know whether this is a book they'd like to have on their shelves, and when we share books with friends, we are giving authors one of the greatest gifts we can give: a word-of-mouth recommendation. A writer is indebted to those who pass along their book with a genuine "You should read this." Thank you!

Acknowledgments

This book has been a colorful labor of love for me and my team. Many thanks go to:

Ben, who supports me in every way, including letting me just be silent when I need to work something out even when he wants nothing more than to talk.

J, A, H, Z, B, Ash, who continue to fill my life with color and inspire so much of my writing.

The Zoombies, who keep me focusing on the good in every color that comes.

Mary Oliver, whose words live on and still inspire me to be a better poet.

Mrs. Jimerson, who still encourages me to write like she knows I can and recognized way back in high school.

Members of the poetry community, who provide a safe place to try out new ideas.

You, dear reader. Thank you for picking up this book. I hope you embrace every color of your life—and you live it to the fullest.

Enjoy more titles from Rachel Toalson

racheltoalson.com

Rachel Toalson Poetry
Starter Library

Enjoy more of Rachel Toalson's poetry with these free downloads.

To get your FREE books, visit *
RachelToalson.com/FreeBook

*Must be 13 or older to be eligible

www.ingramcontent.com/pod-product-compliance
Lightning Source LLC
Chambersburg PA
CBHW060520080526
44586CB00012B/548